COUCH FICTION

A GRAPHIC TALE OF PSYCHOTHERAPY

STORY **PHILIPPA PERRY** ART **JUNKO GRAAT**

AFTERWORD **ANDREW SAMUELS**

palgrave
macmillan

PALGRAVE MACMILLAN
4 Crinan Street, London N1 9XW

Palgrave® and Macmillan® are registered trademarks in the United States,
the United Kingdom, Europe and other countries.

ISBN-13: 978-0-230-25203-5

This book is printed on paper suitable for recycling and made from fully
managed and sustained forest sources. Logging, pulping and manufacturing
processes are expected to conform to the environmental regulations of the
country of origin.

A catalogue record for this book is available from the British Library.
A catalog record for this book is available from the Library of Congress.

Project editor Charlotte Troy
Produced for Palgrave by CT Bureau Ltd. www.ctbureau.co.uk
Printed and bound in Italy by Graphicom on Recycled paper

FOR GRAYSON
AND FLO

Philippa

FOR CHRIS

Junko

NOTE TO THE READER

I wanted to call this book *Interruptions of Contact* but the publisher quite rightly pointed out that it sounded obscure, negative and could be mistaken for coitus interruptus, so we went for *Couch Fiction* instead.

However, what I was trying to imply with the title, 'Interruptions of Contact' was a nod to the phrase used in psychotherapy, 'interruptions to contact' which refers to how we avoid having full contact with others, with ourselves and with the environment, resulting in avoidance of those feelings that full contact would have given. A neurosis can develop and grow if we are not aware of how we interrupt our contact with the world. Sometimes we think we are having a relationship with another, when actually we are mostly having that relationship in our heads as we largely have avoided contact with the other person or thing. If we continue to follow such a pattern, we will develop a neurosis and diminish our experience of being alive.

The habit of avoiding contact and avoiding feelings is usually a creative adaptation to the environment we experienced as children, enabling us to survive and thrive despite less than perfect conditions. However, when the conditions change, we are usually stuck with the old habits even though it may not be in our or the world's best interests to continue with them. This is the underlying theme to the following tale.

With their permission, I have taken content from real people's actual dreams, but apart from that, this story is entirely from my imagination. Although none of the characters have ever existed, nor have any of the events described actually happened, it is typical of psychotherapy case studies. I wrote the book because I wanted to describe what life can be like as a therapist and as a client.

With most of the pictures there are some notes. You can disregard these and still follow the story. Or, if you want to find out more, try the notes.

—Philippa Perry

COUCH FICTION

A GRAPHIC TALE OF PSYCHOTHERAPY

Some schools of psychotherapy suggest that prior to a session, a therapist should empty themselves of preconceptions in order to maintain the openness of mind necessary to be aware of the nuances of the encounter. The psychoanalyst Wilfred Bion said that the therapist must prioritise perception and attention over memory and knowledge as the practitioner's most basic working orientation.

This position is almost always adhered to by the most experienced therapists (occasionally due to dementia rather than a rigid adherence to theory). The therapist in this story is not rigidly adhering to this theory. She is not a perfect therapist and there is no such thing.

I wonder how much research has been done on the impact of recycling bins and their contents on the doorsteps of therapists' premises? I would be especially interested to know of their impact on the first-time client.

Many psychotherapists do not worry about the impression that their appearance makes on their clients*; some have a habit of wearing open-toed orthopaedic sandals whatever the weather. Footwear can give an idea of whether a therapist is working from home or renting a room – slippers or open-toed sandals in winter are a sure sign they are home based.

*This is either because they have worked through their own narcissism issues or they are inherently unstylish, or both.

We can never assume that the absolute truth in and of another person can ever be completely known. It is, however, important in psychotherapy to strive for that truth. Whether Pat clocking that she finds James attractive can be seen as striving for absolute truth is debatable.

COUCH FICTION

In the past, unlike Pat, many therapists didn't ask questions in order to be a blank screen onto which the client then projects. Projection is when instead of having pure contact with another, we project a part of ourselves onto the other person and relate to our own projected part, rather than, or as well as, to the person before us. It is now recognised that a practitioner who says nothing is anything but blank and, however talkative or silent she is, the client will still react to her as she is in the present (with her funny sandals and her recycling).

Nor will failing to remain silent prevent projection or transference. Transference is when we make subconcious assumptions about the person before us in the present, based on our experience of people we have known in the past. For the record, countertransference is what therapists call the feelings that the client causes to emerge in the therapist. It is desirable that therapists recognise their countertransference so as not to complicate an already complicated matter.

By talking about Simon, James is avoiding the subject it would better serve him to talk about – himself. Pat appears to be experiencing a countertransferential parallel process to James, as she too is finding it hard staying with the business in hand. Possibly, due her distraction, Pat has missed the clue that James 'heard' Simon talking about her, rather than James reporting having a conversation he had with Simon. It is as though he has taken the information from Simon by stealth. She missed this. It does not matter. If it is important that a behavioural pattern is addressed, the client will invariably either demonstrate it again, or bring it up later on.

Research has shown that clients are most likely to make positive changes in therapy when the therapist uses the client's own theory of change, or when the therapist's own ideas about change coincide with the client's previously held psychic beliefs. This is why Pat asks James what would work for him.

The highest indicator for a successful outcome for therapy is the client's expectations, motivation and hope. The second is the relationship between the client and the therapist. Neither area seems to be thriving for Pat and James at this stage in the therapy.

Many clients report that naming the issue that brings them to therapy out loud
for the first time can be a powerful experience, even overwhelming.

Psychotherapists are often asked whether it is boring listening to people talk about themselves all day long. The answer is no, not when they are really talking about themselves. If the therapist does feel bored, she will be interested in that feeling because it will be telling her what needs to be addressed in the session is probably not being attended to.

Therapy can break down if client and therapist have not agreed goals. By asking James what he wants, Pat is beginning to negotiate a potential contract for their work together. She is also checking out whether she would be willing to work with James. Not many therapists want to act just as a confessor.

Many people consider undergoing therapy only as a last resort. They have usually tried various strategies to change or to feel better before getting help. Pat would not want to suggest something James has already tried, hence her line of enquiry.

Although kleptomania isn't a particularly common compulsion amongst people in a position to afford private psychotherapy, it is not unusual in that most of us continue with a habit we would rather we didn't. For example: procrastination, smoking, eating too much, being over critical, over-reacting, acting shy, getting drunk… the list goes on.

Inevitably when a therapist looks back over a session, there is always something she could have done more sensitively or intelligently. Here, Pat is going too fast for James in looking for triggers for his behaviour. It would serve him better at this stage if she empathised with him more. The idea, though, is not to be perfect. The idea is to remain authentic while striving for the unknowable truth.

I SAW THIS OLIVE OIL.
I DIDN'T THINK ABOUT IT.
I CERTAINLY DIDN'T NEED IT.
I JUST TOOK IT AND...

...PUT IT IN MY
BRIEFCASE AND
CLOSED IT.

SHE CAME BACK WITH
THE OLIVES, I PAID FOR
THEM AND LEFT.

If this was an ordinary conversation and not a therapy session, Pat would probably go into raptures about the combination of pitted black olives in chilli oil with pickled garlic available at the nearby Spanish deli. But this isn't an ordinary conversation and so she does not share her passion about olives with James. Although James is relating a story about buying olives, olives are obviously not the subject here.

The process of telling the story and the relationship of the teller to the story is of more interest to a therapist than the content of the story itself. The content is the icing but the process is the cake itself. This is why therapists will often ask a client how they feel about the story they've just told. It is another of the differences between a normal conversation and a therapy session.

Pat is formulating theories about James' behaviour that she is choosing not to share. Therapists commonly refer to this process as 'bracketing'. Pat does not know James very well yet, so she is unsure about what he can and cannot tolerate hearing at this stage. Possibly it would serve James better if she also bracketed her line of enquiry about triggers, as her inability to let go of the trigger theme is in danger of rupturing their relationship.

Bracketing is more complex than just withholding information. It actually means suspending judgment. To understand this thoroughly one has to study the philosophy of Husserl. He talked a lot about how seeing a horse qualifies as a horsiness experience irrespective of whether the horse appears in reality, in a dream or hallucination. He also talked about the very essence of how you experience the phenomenon of horse essence, but I'll bracket that.

Pat continues to pursue her trigger theory. Her speed here means that she doesn't stay in contact with James. In her enthusiasm, she appears to have forgotten her early counselling training on closely tracking the client and going at the client's pace. James is being pushed not only to where he does not want to go, but where his body is unwilling to go, and so he goes blank. Going blank, or dissociating, is not an act of will but an automatic response to certain stimuli.

Some people are more prone to this response than others, especially if they started to do it at a very young age. You might assume – and perhaps this is Pat's mistake – that James being a highly educated professional person would be able to follow Pat's simple questioning. But all of us have the potential to be highly functioning in some areas and relatively immature in others.

In most people's lives, there are three main areas: what we do, where we live and who we live with. Pat has tried the first area, what we do – work, in other words – and did not come up with anything. She's moved on to the people in his life to see if anything untoward is happening there.

Therapy is not like a normal conversation in that there can be long silences in order to give things time to emerge from the unconscious mind into awareness. Although unless this has been previously negotiated between the parties, what is likely to come up is, 'Why isn't she saying anything?' or 'What am I supposed to do now?'

As either a client or a therapist, if something pops into your mind, it may be worth sharing. Even if, on your own, you cannot see its relevance.

Here, Pat is voicing a hunch. Sometimes a therapist's hunches come to nothing and sometimes they are useful.

Smugness is not attractive in anyone and is certainly not helpful in a psychothera-pist. However, it is a human, authentic response. There is a lot of debate in the profession about therapists' personal disclosure of feelings. It is posited that even if it is desirable for the therapist to keep their emotional response to themselves, this is impossible to do as it will be picked up by the client anyway.

PAT TAKES A POTTED LIFE HISTORY FROM JAMES. HIS FATHER RECENTLY RETIRED AS A STOCKBROKER AND HIS MOTHER DABBLED IN INTERIOR DESIGN. HE GREW UP IN SURBURAN SURREY IN A LARGE HOUSE WITH A COUPLE OF ACRES. HE WENT TO PUBLIC SCHOOL AND THEN TO ONE OF THE OLDER UNIVERSITIES. NOW HE IS A SUCCESSFUL BARRISTER PRACTISING COMMERCIAL PROPERTY LAW.

WE'LL STOP HERE FOR NOW. DO YOU WANT TO CARRY ON COMING TO SEE ME?

I'LL TRY A FEW MORE SESSIONS. WILL I BE CURED?

WHAT AM I LETTING MYSELF IN FOR?

I CAN GIVE NO GUARANTEES THAT YOU'LL BE CURED.

SHE HASN'T DONE A MARKETING COURSE.

It might seem strange to a novice therapist or layperson why Pat feels trepidation about taking on James as a client. It is because in order for therapy to work, she will need to involve herself at an emotional level and that means actually struggling with the patient and with herself. It is not a light undertaking.

Personally, I am wary of therapists who have done a marketing course, give guarantees and promise great results from 'ground-breaking' techniques. What works in therapy is a motivated client, a good therapeutic alliance and hope. A logo, a motto and having to pay in advance are no substitute for recommendation, reputation, relationship and trust.

There is no point in banging on to clients about the relationship between client and therapist being the most important factor in successful psychotherapy. Frankly, it sounds creepy. Either it will become apparent or the therapy will flounder anyway.

Therapists have done a fine job of convincing clients that conditions ('boundaries') are for the benefit of the client. They may well may be and I think therapists need to be challenged about them periodically.

By putting aside her usual rule of being paid at the time of the session, Pat is demonstrating a genuine willingness to place James' interests before her own. Such a move may facilitate the forming of a bond between Pat and James. Or it may even be a corrective emotional experience for James. He has been courageous enough to confess his failing and to feel the shame of having done so.

Pat's practical kindness could be seen, or unconsciously felt by James, as Pat also being willing to be affected by him and accepting of him. On the other hand, boundary breaking by the therapist is very much frowned upon in the psychotherapeutic profession as being unprofessional and potentially harmful to the client. One thing is for sure, nothing is certain.

Why do most therapists ask about childhood? If childhood conditions aren't optimal, the creative part of the child develops a strategic pattern of behaviour to circumnavigate the less-than-perfect conditions. These self-protective strategies can become habitual. If and when the circumstances of a person's life change and their habits do not, the self-protective strategies can become self-destructive strategies. Some theorists argue that it is unnecessary to dig up the past and that they can make a client feel better just by working in the here and now. The trouble with these working-only-in-the-present approaches tends to be that, although a client can be trained to control their symptoms, because the underlying causes are not necessarily addressed, the client can develop a new set of symptoms. For example, a person with selective mutism is trained to talk but she then goes on to develop chronic constipation. I suggest that this is because the original trauma that caused the mutism was not addressed so her withholding pattern found another way to present. Therapies that address only symptoms and not causes are a bit like putting a plaster on an uncleaned wound. At first the plaster stops the flow of blood, but unless it's taken off and what is underneath is attended to, there is a risk of gangrene.

There are schools of therapy that exhort that the therapist should use the client's terms of reference and style wherever possible. There are others that insist that the practitioner is always a hundred per cent authentic and centred in themselves.

Every exchange in every session is a choice point for the therapist. It is fortunate that there is almost always more than one appropriate response that the therapist could make.

Pat will be holding in mind here the usual belief held by psychotherapists that people are not born obnoxious or defensive, but were trained to be that way in their childhood and by other formative experiences. Ideally, she would be able to raise his awareness of his annoying behaviour in a way unlikely to shame him. The theory is that this can be done by identifying and empathising with the feeling underlying the undesirable behaviour. A lot of psychotherapy is about striving to make an effective, non-shaming intervention but striving for something does not mean you'll succeed. In our example, Pat's intention is good but, unfortunately, her intervention causes James to feel shame that causes him to go momentarily blank.

Although her previous response had been clumsy, James must have felt her genuine honesty and his next defense is a non-aggressive attempt at humour as he takes on the role of a told-off little boy. Pat takes the little boy act seriously. She has read her Freud and is taking his line here that there is no such thing as a joke.

She also knows she should investigate the feelings behind this defensive behaviour. But Pat tends to go too fast so she disregards his possible discomfort and ploughs straight in.

According to Attachment Theory, people who describe their childhoods as 'perfect' were not securely attached to their primary care-giver. Taking their cue from this first relationship, subsequent relationships can be problematic. Those who had 'good enough' mothers, who were able to form a functioning bond with their child, have a more balanced view. They can afford to see that there are bad bits as well as good bits in their childhoods. This is why in psychotherapy school, all therapists are fitted with a Perfect Childhood Alarm. It can be a heart sinking moment for a therapist when it starts to ring. Insecurely attached infants go on to develop patterns of attachment in adulthood that don't necessarily give them the best chance of fulfilling their potential for happiness. These patterns have been identified and have labels. The four main categories are: Dismissing, Preoccupied, Avoidant and Unresolved/Disorganised. If upon further investigation, you find yourself fitting into one of these categories, do not despair, healthier patterns can be learnt.

Here, James is hiding his issues behind his denials. If I say to you, 'Don't think about oranges', the 'oranges' would be the issue and the 'don't', the denial. And by saying, 'Don't think about oranges', I will have unwittingly brought oranges to your mind. James' issue is his vague 'bad', which he prefixes with 'nothing' – his denial. He mentions 'split up' which he tries to push away with 'didn't'. And 'my universe ... fell apart', he tempers with 'never'. So unwittingly, James has begun to share with Pat some of his formative experience. It seems that Pat might be feeling some of the impact of these early experiences. When one person denies their bad feeling, it may be felt by the other. This is called projective identification.

In order to get James to be realistic about his childhood, Pat asks for a specific example. The picture James paints is of a child opening presents by himself. He doesn't talk about his own experience but relates the family story that exists around it. He has probably unknowingly taken this as his own experience and laughs along with it like the originators of the myth did.

Pat does not feel able to mirror James' smile at this point, nor is she able to feel his joy – a possible indication that there is no joy to be felt. We all need a 'secure base' to run to when the going gets tough. The way James is talking, it is likely that he feels his 'secure base' is in things, rather than people.

It could be sheer coincidence that James finds himself talking about something precious that died through lack of care and attention. It would certainly be dangerous to make any assumption that his unconscious is painting a more accurate picture of his childhood than the one he is aware of trying to impart to Pat.

Pat is making an effort to listen to all of James, even those parts of James that he isn't aware of. It is possibly too early in their relationship for her to share some of what she is hearing and her mistimed question causes James to get more defensive.

It is important for a therapist not to have too much of her own agenda. James does not want to think that his childhood was anything less than perfect and Pat has no truck with this so it feels here as though they could have reached a stalemate. Intersubjectivity theory argues that the therapist's and the client's subjective views are equal and neither one right nor wrong. The idea is that Pat could gently investigate the fears behind James' stance, while she imagines what it might feel like for him, rather than trying to change his mind to fit in with her perspective. However, it seems at the moment that Pat has forgotten about intersubjectivity theory.

It appears from James' memory that his mother might have used him to bolster her own sense of importance. James can see nothing wrong with the picture and he remains defensive.

At last, Pat has let go of her agenda and starts to investigate feelings, her own as well as James'. She describes the atmosphere as she experiences it, which is probably permission-giving to James to state what he is feeling.

Perhaps as Pat is concentrating on how James feels, rather than trying to force him where he doesn't want to go, he opens up a little…

When psychotherapists work, they are supposed to be thoughtful, reflective and responsible and track the client sensitively and only offer well-timed nudges that tie in to the stage the client is at. I think inexperienced psychotherapists can be better at this than old hands. Older, experienced therapists have seen it all before, gone to many conferences, written academic papers, read academic papers and practised for tens of thousands of hours. Therefore sometimes going slowly, at the new client's pace, isn't their bag. Pat is thinking about feeding, which probably means she has missed that she has got some sort of mother bird counter-transference going on and is about to act on it.

What Pat is doing here is sharing her belief system with James. James' reaction is to dissociate. Sometimes when a person dissociates, they split into another state, like another personality. James, the adult, appears to have blanked off but there seems to be a five- or six-year-old boy that is listening to some of what she is saying. However, since she isn't tailoring her approach to a young boy, James cannot understand, or even hear much of what she says.

All of us dissociate to some extent and some of us do split off into an earlier version of ourselves which is the part that was traumatised by a previous event or by an ongoing traumatising relationship. Some people split into several different versions of themselves or even appear to become different people. We all have the capacity to do this and maybe all do it to a greater or lesser extent. In its more extreme form, it is called Dissociative Identity Disorder. It used to be known as Multiple Personality Disorder.

Like all therapists, Pat's interventions can be clumsy but due to her experience and her belief that she knows what she is doing, she conveys a sense to James of her own confidence in her methods.

On this page, Pat and James are having one of their rare meetings of minds, due to James' five-year-old self feeling understood by Pat.

There are various theories about the stages of therapy. One system terms these: pre-contemplation; contemplation; preparation; action; maintenance and termination. Another system calls the stages: consciousness raising; dramatic relief; environmental re-evaluation; self-reevaluation; self-liberation; counter-conditioning; contingency management; stimulus control; helping relationships.

My favourite is Bruce Tuckman's. He designed it to describe the life of groups but it can also be applied to groups of two: forming; norming; storming; performing; and adjourning. Pat and James are currently at the norming stage of their relationship.

It appears that Pat has reflected on her work with James. She may even have had some supervision on this case (supervision is a statutory requirement for most therapists' professional bodies). She seems to have realised that no amount of 'feeding' will expedite James to where he needs to be. So she is biding her time and has minimised her challenges. She allows him to describe his childhood as 'great'.

By allowing James to work at his own pace, he can feel behind his own breakthroughs.

People sometimes ask me whether the use of dreams in therapy is nothing more than an old cliché and what use can they possibly be? The masters were very lyrical on this point: Freud described dreams as the 'Royal Road to the Unconscious' and Fritz Perls called them 'The Royal Road to Integration'. My belief about dreams is that the language part of our brain is not necessarily the part where many of our actions emanate from. It is good to have a look at other parts of ourselves which may motivate and which haven't got a direct language link to our conscious side. But then I am not much of a poet.

NO PAT, I DON'T. THAT'S ODD ISN'T IT?

WHAT COMES UP FOR YOU IF YOU THINK AROUND THAT?

ON THE WAY HERE I NIPPED INTO A SHOP TO BUY A BANANA. THERE WAS A MUM WITH A SMALL BOY. HE POINTED TO SOME SWEETS AND SHE SAID, 'NO'. HE WHIMPERED A BIT, THEN SHE TOLD HIM OFF FOR WHIMPERING AND HE STARTED TO SCREAM ... WHY AM I THINKING ABOUT THIS?

COULD HE BE YOU? YOU'VE HAD A BAD DREAM. YOU WHIMPER, YOU TELL YOURSELF OFF FOR WHIMPERING, THEN POSSIBLY YOU FEEL WORSE...

I SUPPOSE THE MUM WASN'T THAT SYMPATHETIC TO THE KID'S FRUSTRATION. I DON'T EXPECT ... ER ...

... ER ... OTHER PEOPLE ... YOU ... TO BE SYMPATHETIC ABOUT MY NIGHTMARE BUT I SUPPOSE IT'S ME WHO'S SAYING IT'S NOT THAT BAD AND IT WAS YOU WHO POINTED OUT THAT IT WAS ME WHO DIDN'T EXPECT TO BE TAKEN SERIOUSLY. SHALL I TELL YOU THAT DREAM NOW?

GOOD, YES.

James is 'free associating' here – a good old Freudian technique whereby the therapist instructs the client to ponder around something and then describe the first thing that comes up to the surface. It can shed light on the dark recesses of the unconscious mind. There is an intervention around the subject of entitlement to feelings that many therapists like to pop into every client's therapy at some point. It is the 'Two Things to Cry About Intervention'. It is this: you feel sad about something, you tell yourself off for feeling sad about it, then you feel even worse.

The reason for feeling even worse is that you have two things to cry about: the original hurt and the hurt you feel because you are telling yourself off. After hearing this explanation for why they feel so terrible, clients are supposed to feel much better because hopefully they then revert back to only having one thing to cry about. However, if it doesn't work, you may end up with three. Pat is trying to give the Two Things to Cry About Intervention but James can interpret what has come up from the free association for himself and Pat is learning to accept James' reality.

LAST NIGHT I DREAMT I WAS BACK AT SCHOOL.

IT WAS MY KINDERGARTEN, EXCEPT IT WAS ON CRAGGY ROCKS.

I THOUGHT I'D FALL OFF THE ROCKS.

THEN AN ANGEL CAME TO GET ME – ALTHOUGH SHE WAS AN ANGEL, I KNOW SHE WAS MY MOTHER.

... SHE HAD NO FACE – I DIDN'T NOTICE THAT AT FIRST BUT WHEN I DID, IT WAS SCARIER THAN HER BEING LATE.

When we try telling or re-telling a dream, quite often details we did not notice the first time will come back to us. Is this because we are re-stimulating the dreaming part of the brain and it is re-sending the message it wanted us to get the first time? Or are we just remembering better?

It seems that Pat has missed a possible line of enquiry here. Maybe Marta's leaving is significant? Perhaps James projects Marta onto Juanita? And perhaps it does not matter that Pat has not followed this up because some of our unconscious enactments work just fine for us.

When people undergo psychotherapy, it is uncanny how relevant memories find their way to the surface and dreams provide more information than a client may have realised they had access to. It is as though humans have an inner drive to fulfill their potential. Humanistic psychotherapists refer to this as the 'self-actualisation' drive.

There are two types of questions: open questions (for example: 'What are you feeling?') and closed questions to which the answer can usually only be 'yes' or 'no' (for instance: 'Are you feeling happy?'). Therapy students are steered away from closed questioning as it can close down a line of enquiry rather than open it up.

Pat has a weakness for asking questions that fish for specific answers. Her first one misses and her second one is timely. Even in the smoothest therapy, there are plenty of misses. The process of missing and then readjusting is sometimes known as 'rupture and repair'.

This is an example of a relevant memory taking its time to surface. It is not that James will have been deliberately withholding this memory. Sometimes I imagine we have an internal security department that makes decisions on when to release memories dependent upon what support systems we have in place.

It is very common that when parents start to have problems with their relationship, a child will unconsciously play up or sometimes get ill. Such a creative coping strategy of childhood can become a lifelong habit.

It might appear contra-indicated for a recovering addict to talk about the advantages of his compulsion. Yet in my clinical experience, unless the thrills as well as the spills are consciously known about, it is harder for a client to get behind his decision to stop. By acknowledging the benefits of an addiction, we are then able to seek alternative ways to gain those advantages.

In order to keep the client talking, one of the first interventions the student therapist learns is to repeat the last phrase that he said before going silent. It's a winner. It can also be used to draw out shy guests at dinner parties. In the example here, it nudges James' split off part, little James, into action.

A part of the 'flight or fight' response is the freeze response. If we keep as still as possible by not breathing, or breathing as shallowly as we can, we are less likely to be seen or heard by a possible predator. I don't think that James believes that Pat will literally eat him. Not breathing is more of an involuntary response due to his fear of feeling. Pat doesn't get James to breathe in order to make him feel terrible. She wants him to discover that his feelings will not harm him, unlike what he might do to avoid them, which could.

Pat and James have formed (said hello), normed (got used to each other) and
now it seems they might be at the storming stage of their relationship.

It is gratifying for a therapist when their client, who used to repress feelings, allows himself to feel. However, anger can raise the therapist's heart rate a little. Pat self-soothes well by using her name to herself and geeing herself up.

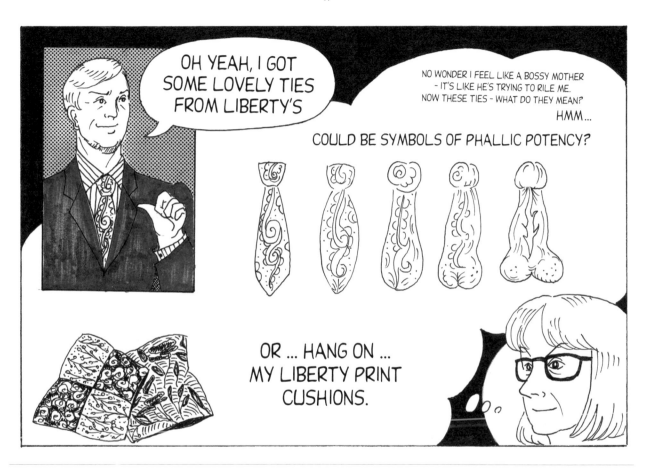

Luckily, Pat manages to bracket her 'phallic potency' interpretation.

In a normal conversation, as opposed to a therapy conversation, Pat might very well continue to argue, but it would not help James if she did and her job is to help James. As she is managing her countertransference, she manages to stop defending herself and return instead to focused, crisp enquiry.

WITH ME?

SUPPOSE SO.

WHEN DID YOU KNOW YOU WERE ANGRY WITH ME? BEFORE YOU WENT TO LIBERTY'S?

AFTERWARDS ... ONLY NOW REALLY.

IT MIGHT BE HORRIBLE HAVING FEELINGS, BUT SHUTTING THEM DOWN AND THEN ACTING OUT ON THEM MAY NOT BE YOUR BEST POLICY.

I'LL TAKE THE BLOODY TIES BACK OR PAY FOR THEM.

Pat is right. If we do repress feelings, they can find other ways to surface, but explaining this to James at this point is slightly mistimed, as he seems to have heard it more as a telling off and he reacts in a surly manner.

Pat is sufficiently secure at this stage in their therapeutic alliance to call it a 'relationship' and to talk about their relationship being a useful tool in the therapy without it sounding too weird. At least, she doesn't think it sounds weird.

Yes, clients do need to be warned that sometimes they might feel worse before
they feel better – and even that they might never feel better.

Pat could have argued here that she did not warn him for his own good because she was afraid that, had she done so, he would not have had the benefit of therapy. Fortunately, she does not go down this path because sanctimonious therapy never cured anyone of anything. She even tells him why he is right.

A popular misconception is that hypnosis is a form of unconsciousness resembling sleep. Actually it is a wakeful state of heightened suggestibility combined with diminished peripheral awareness. Pat does not know whether James is in this state of focused attention but she might be aware that her calm assurance delivered with authority and certainty could have a positive effect.

85

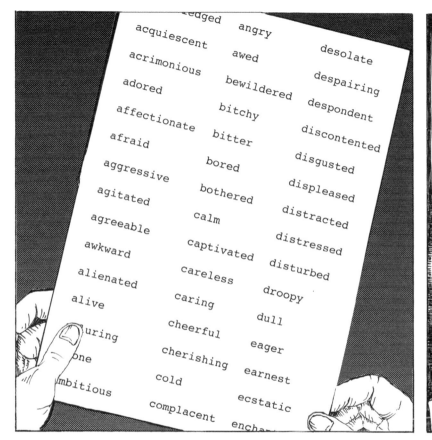

Pat remembers to ask James about feelings and gets him to further define them. It can be important to know how we physically recognise different emotions to increase our awareness of them, thus minimising the dangers of unconscious enactments.

When Freud and a patient made a breakthrough, they often paused for a celebratory cigar to let the realisation sink in, but that is not Pat's style.

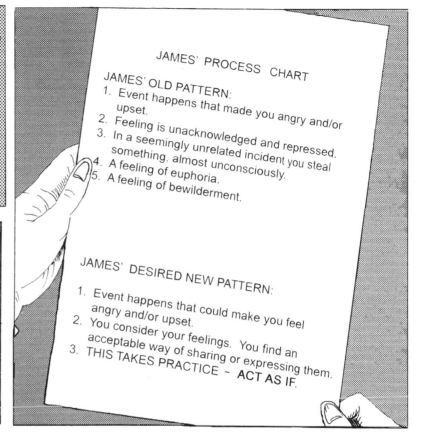

By giving James a chart of his behavioural patterns, Pat hopes to consolidate the work they have done together to help James become more aware of how his stealing behaviour is triggered. She is also purveying the age-old tradition of the Healing Ritual. Healing rituals have been firmly established as a part of healing since the concept of healing first arrived. Other examples of healing rituals are: the doctor's ward round; the analyst's couch; the prescription; etc. When a practitioner really believes in their procedures, research has shown that the ensuing cure is as likely due to a placebo effect as the medicine or exercise prescribed.

If a therapist prescribes an exercise, it is more likely to succeed if the practitioner follows it up. By setting homework and asking about it, she is conveying her hope and expectation of improvement and therefore gives the exercise and its placebo effect the best chance of success.

I REALISED THAT I WASN'T FEELING ANYTHING.

AND THAT THIS WAS TYPICAL OF SITUATIONS WHERE I DON'T ALLOW MYSELF TO FEEL.

AND THESE ARE?

SITUATIONS WHERE MANY PEOPLE WOULD PROBABLY GET ANGRY, I GO BLANK. THIS WAS THE FIRST TIME I'VE NOTICED THE BLANKING.

I WAS AWARE I DIDN'T FEEL ANYTHING AS I ROUTINELY DEALT WITH THE SMASHED WINDOW.

I CAUGHT MYSELF DISMISSING THE SENSE I HAD OF HAVING HAD MY SPACE VIOLATED. I NOTICED I TRIED TO CONVINCE MYSELF THAT THE WASTE OF TIME AND MONEY WAS NO BIG DEAL AS I REPLACED STOLEN CDS.

In the 1960s, therapists used to get clients to express their anger by thumping cushions. Pat hasn't used that intervention since experimenting with it on an early counselling course but it seems that James has found it by himself.

 WHAT WAS GOING THROUGH YOUR MIND IN THE GYM WHILE YOU WERE PUNCHING?

 I PRETENDED THE PUNCH BAG WAS THE FACELESS THUG WHO SMASHED MY CAR, INVADED MY SPACE, TOOK MY STUFF.

 WHAM! I GAVE HIM WHAT FOR.

 WERE YOU CROSS WITH JUANITA WITH LIVING WHERE SHE DOES?

 THAT'S NOT HER FAULT.

 FEELINGS AREN'T NECESSARILY LOGICAL OR JUSTIFIABLE.

BUT BEING AWARE OF FEELINGS, BRINGING THEM INTO YOUR CONSCIOUSNESS, MAY GIVE YOU MORE CHOICE AS TO WHETHER YOU ACT OUT ON THEM OR NOT.

I wonder if it is easier for James to take on board Pat's theorising, now she has allowed herself to see more from James' point of view? Clinical qualitative research argues, yes.

There is a difference between saying 'feel about coming here' and 'feel about our relationship'. The latter is more to the point and can be more difficult to say. When there does not seem to be language to describe a feeling, it is useful to see what metaphors come to mind. Language mainly emanates from the left hemisphere of the brain and dreaming, feeling and creativity mainly come from the right, so if one is not sure how one feels about something, let go of trying too hard to calculate it (calculations are mainly left-brain) and see if a metaphorical picture comes to mind instead.

If this was an analysis rather than psychotherapy, Pat and James may have looked at the significance of James' transference and Pat's countertransference and any links between them in more detail. But psychotherapy has more emphasis on the relationship between the client and the therapist, rather than working with just the transference. Pat is more concerned with their contract for the session, which is for James to put into words how he feels about Juanita. So Pat picks up on what James is trying to say about his relationship with Pat in order that he can practise his articulation about feelings towards another on her. She seems to miss the sexual overtone of his transference. And I'll say it again, if an issue isn't picked up by the therapist the first time a client hints at it, he will inevitably bring it up again.

... LOVE COMING HERE.

I LOOK FORWARD TO WORKING WITH YOU TOO.

IT'S WEIRD, STEALING HAS STOPPED WORKING FOR ME. I THINK THAT WAS WHAT MADE ME ANGRY WITH YOU. YOU ALLOWED ME TO EXPLORE THAT RAGE AND I'VE NEVER FELT SUCH PERMISSION TO BE MYSELF. NOW I FEEL, ER UM, MORE OKAY WITH MYSELF. SO THANK YOU PAT. I THINK YOU ARE GREAT.

IS THIS IDEALISED TRANSFERENCE OR SHOULD I ENJOY A COMPLIMENT? UM

UM ... YOU'VE SHOWN PART OF YOURSELF THAT YOU'VE KEPT HIDDEN FOR A LONG TIME. YOU'VE ACCEPTED THAT PART OF YOU NOW. YOU DID THAT WORK. FEELING OKAY IS YOUR DOING.

An idealised transference is when the therapist is seen as being perfect and brilliant and we know and Pat knows that she is not that. She is afraid that James may be viewing her through an idealised lens, like he did his own childhood. People who are learning not to idealise their parents can be vulnerable because they can easily carry on the idealising, and merely switch the object of their idolatry (cults rely on this).

It is also undesirable for a client to project his shining light onto the therapist instead of owning it for himself. If Pat does not challenge him when he may be idealising, it will eventually hinder his recovery. So Pat points out how he has helped himself so he doesn't believe all his personal development is entirely down to her. At the same time, she is careful not to deny his reality or his effect on how she feels about herself.

It is probably important that James looks at his sexual feelings towards Pat as he has bought up the subject again. Unlike on page 98, this time Pat notices.

It isn't easy to find a universally causal explanation for erotic transference. All emotional states are multi-determined. But it is usually possible and desirable to look at the process and dynamic behind the content of any sexual fantasy a client has for a therapist in order to understand what might be being enacted in that fantasy. If the therapist does not give an interpretation for the sexualised transference, the therapy can reach an impasse.

Pat can sense that James does indeed have a sexual fantasy about her and that it may not be the one he has presented. In my clinical practice, I have noticed that if I ask a client to make up a dream if they can't remember one, or to fantasise a scenario, what they come up with, as often as not, is their usual formula – their usual pattern. In both of James' fantasies, the one he shares and the one he keeps private, their roles of recipient and giver are reversed. She is either the one begging for sex or needing comfort and he is the provider in both scenarios. Pat therefore does not need to embarrass James by insisting on the truth. The fantasy he came up with on the spur of the moment holds enough truth for them to work on.

Even though, like the majority of suppliers and users of privately funded psycho-therapy, both Pat and James are white and middle class, there are still, even in that narrow field, differences that it may be beneficial to explore.

Pat offers an interpretation that makes sense to James and he is able to return to the business of how to woo Juanita and why it might be so uncomfortable to fail.

James' judgement actually sounds sensible and it might have appeared reasonable to leave it there when he became aware of his immature need to have his own way. However, it is often a good idea to put a judgement to one side and have a look to see what is behind the behaviour that it is tempting merely to judge. Unless root causes of undesirable behaviour are discovered it quite often happens that the root cause will find a new outlet that might also be undesirable.

Pat is speeding away as usual, but unlike the early sessions of this therapy relationship now they are speeding along together. It can be quite dangerous to ask a client to speculate about what another person in his life might be feeling or thinking, because the idea is to get clients to own their own feelings and to have real contactful relationships with others, rather than non-contactful relationships with what they merely imagine the other to feel. Pat has asked him to think about Juanita's feelings in case he is harbouring an assumption that needs to be challenged.

He was indeed harbouring an assumption that needed to be challenged. Another assumption often made is that therapists and analysts never give advice.

James is displaying a value judgement here based on the appearance of things. It is as if he only knows how impressive or otherwise things are because of the ideas he has assigned to those things, rather than his actual experience of those things. By bringing this subject up now, or rather by talking in this style, it is as though James wants to tackle his narcissism.

Clerkenwell is a trendy area of London comprising designer lofts and gentrified Georgian houses, desirable restaurants, boutiques, galleries, and proximity to the City and West End. Elephant and Castle is a poorer area comprising public housing, the cheapest chain stores, discount shops and a higher crime rate. However it is possible to be happy or miserable in either borough.

Pat seems to have realised, perhaps only unconsciously, that James' first port of call is his relationship with things rather than people, so she frames her question in a way that invites him to talk about the objects in Juanita's flat.

It is a measure of how much James trusts Pat that he is able to admit that his house is designed primarily to make an impression. He understands that he inherited this value system from his parents without question.

This way of imbibing a belief system whole without chewing it over, or questioning it, is called introjection.

The effect of Pat asking James what he values in Juanita will compound the new value system he has discovered within himself. I'm guessing that Pat will only realise this with the benefit of hindsight when she reviews the session, but it could have been a conscious decision on her part to distance him further from a narcissistic value system.

James started the session with a narcissistic theme, as though settling on the subject for his session, and has sufficient ego strength to assert himself to return to it when Pat starts to deviate.

Living in a narcissistic world is like living in a bubble. If that bubble is popped and there is no support system to hold the narcissist, it can be devastating. When describing his mother here, James tells of a pattern of a narcissistic 'false self' being built up before being 'popped' again.

James has learnt the therapist's trick of repeating the last two words in order to get the other person to say more.

Pat is talking about 'affect regulation' – how people regulate their feelings. A mother can sooth her infant by attunement and containment, which means taking her infant's feelings seriously, although not dramatically. This gradually teaches the child how to regulate his own feelings for himself. If children do not have the benefit of this type of 'good enough' parenting, it is likely they will have difficulty with self-soothing later in life. They get into hyper-states, which means they cannot calm themselves down, or hypo-states, where they close down too much and go blank and cannot easily rouse themselves. They can also swing from hyper to hypo, or hypo to hyper, without spending much time in the ideal regulated state in the middle. We all have our coping mechanisms which we use to try to keep ourselves in our preferred state. Some of these coping mechanisms are healthier than others. For example, on page 76 Pat used her own name when talking to herself to keep calm in the face of James' anger. This is a healthy way of self-soothing. Had she reached for a bottle of vodka, it would have been less healthy.

It seems likely that James is well into the action stage of his work or, as Tucker would have it, performing.

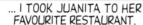

... I TOOK JUANITA TO HER FAVOURITE RESTAURANT.

I TOLD HER THAT I DIDN'T WANT THE EXCITEMENT OF MEETING ONCE OR TWICE A WEEK.

I TOLD HER THAT I WANTED TO WAKE UP TO HER EVERY DAY.

... THAT EVEN THOUGH I DIDN'T SHOW IT, I WAS SAD WHEN SHE HADN'T WANTED TO MOVE IN.

... THAT IT FELT LIKE SHE HADN'T TAKEN ME SERIOUSLY.

I SAID I DIDN'T BLAME HER BECAUSE I HADN'T TAKEN MYSELF SERIOUSLY.

SHE DIDN'T KNOW WHAT I MEANT. SHE ASKED ME FOR MORE DETAILS.

If we look at James' previous report of how he had made proposals to Juanita [pages 31, 106], we'll see that he 'mentioned' to her that she could move in with him. He had not made a declaration of his feelings before.

Some say that practising being open and direct in therapy can train a person to be more open and direct in their lives in general. There are many people, and possibly James was one of them, who are sufficiently assertive at work but, for multi-determined reasons, are less so in their personal lives.

I'M TAKING A BIG RISK HERE. IF SHE REALISES THE SWANKY BARRISTER IS ACTUALLY A THIEF SHE MIGHT LEAVE.

I THOUGHT ABOUT IT.

BUT I TOLD PAT AND SHE STILL TOOK ME ON. IF I WANT A SERIOUS INTIMATE RELATIONSHIP I NEED TO TELL HER.

I THOUGHT SOME MORE.

SO I TOLD JUANITA ABOUT THERAPY AND EVERYTHING.

I FELT SO CLOSE TO HER.

WE WENT FOR A WALK IN THE PARK. WE TALKED ALL NIGHT.

In 1955, two men called Joe and Harry came up with a cognitive tool called the Johari Window [see overleaf]. It consists of a square divided into four squares. The Arena square stands for the parts of ourselves that we see and others see. The Blind Spot square is the aspect that others see but we are not aware of. Façade square is our private space, we are aware of it but others are not. The Unknown square is the most mysterious room in that the unconscious or subconscious bit of us is seen by neither ourselves nor others.

By sharing more of his true self with Juanita, James is making the Arena square a lot larger and therefore the Façade square smaller. If a person takes the risk of making the Arena square bigger, quite often other people follow and enlarge their own Arena squares. This results in greater intimacy [Fig. 2]. This seems to have happened between James and Juanita.

SHE TOLD ME NEW THINGS AS WELL. SHE IS SCARED OF SPIDERS. NOT LIKE A JOKE BUT PROPER ARACHNOPHOBIA. AND SHE WAS ASHAMED SHE FELT LIKE THAT AND THOUGHT I'D THINK LESS OF HER FOR IT.

SHE SAID SHE RINGS HER MUM AND HER SISTERS EVERYDAY, HER DAD EVERY OTHER DAY AND HER COUSINS EVERY WEEK. APPARENTLY HER LAST BOYFRIEND TOLD HER THIS WAS UNNATURAL. BUT SHE SAID SHE LOVES THEM AND LIKES TO HEAR THEIR VOICES.

HELLO

SHE'D NEVER TOLD ME BEFORE BECAUSE SHE THOUGHT I'D HATE THAT. I LOVE IT. SHE SAYS SOMETIMES SHE RINGS THEM FOR A GOOD ARGUMENT. THEY SOUND SUCH A CLOSE FAMILY, I CAN'T WAIT TO MEET THEM. I'VE SIGNED UP FOR SPANISH LESSONS!

For discussion of the Johari Window (pictured here), please see footnote on previous page.

Figure 1:

	KNOWN TO SELF	NOT KNOWN TO SELF
KNOWN TO OTHERS	ARENA	BLIND SPOT
NOT KNOWN TO OTHERS	FAÇADE	UNKNOWN

Figure 2:

	KNOWN TO SELF	NOT KNOWN TO SELF
KNOWN TO OTHERS	ARENA	BLIND SPOT
NOT KNOWN TO OTHERS	FAÇADE	UNKNOWN

What is particularly gratifying in this sequence is that although it shows that James and indeed Juanita are advocates of openness and directness, they are not suggesting that it is necessarily a good thing to spill everything about yourself to a person you do not know.

COUCH FICTION

A heightened sense of feeling and an increased readiness to allow the impact of the good will of strangers are often side effects of having had an intense positive emotional experience. Fathers of newborns often report this type of phenomenon. And/or maybe there is an unconscious parallel between the story he has just told and his psychotherapeutic journey? He couldn't find his way, he asked for help, he found his way. In both instances, he found his way because of a relationship. Had Pat spotted this, I wonder if there would have been any point in her giving James this interpretation?

People usually come to therapy because they don't understand why they feel bad and they want to feel better but don't know how to go about it. To tackle this problem, some psychology researchers feel it is more useful to research positive mental health rather than mental distress. It can be as important to raise our own awareness of how we organise ourselves to feel good as it is to understand how we make ourselves feel the reverse.

I WAS A BOY OF EIGHT OR NINE WHO HARVESTED OYSTERS.

WE LIVED BY A CHUTE WHERE THEY LAUNCHED BOATS INTO WATER.

WE LIVED BY A SORT OF RAMP ...

... WITH BEDS MADE OUT OF SILK AND TREES ...

... AND CARPETS THAT TRAILED INTO THE WATER.

I THOUGHT ABOUT GOING IN BUT MY FRIEND WANTED TO PLAY OUTSIDE.

SO WE DID – THE MUSIC WAS BEAUTIFUL AND THE CARPETS WERE THERE.

WE ROLLED ON THEM – IT WAS DARK AND CALM. AND BEAUTIFUL MUSIC PLAYED ALL THE TIME.

I WOKE UP SO HAPPY, STILL HEARING THE MUSIC IN MY HEAD.

SO WHAT DOES IT MEAN PAT?

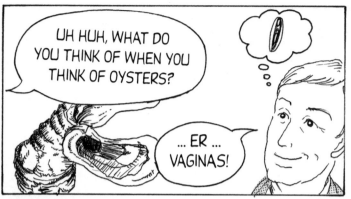

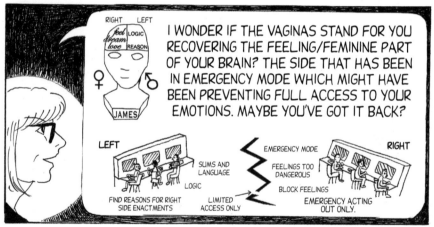

An added benefit of allowing ourselves to feel our sadness, our pain, our existential voids, etc., is that we then have greater access to our sense of humour as well. Therapists' consulting rooms witness laughter as well as tears.

Contrary to what purveyors of New Age dream books would have you believe, there is no universal dream language. There may be similarities in some people's symbolism but it would be erroneous to assume that dreaming of oysters means that you are discovering your feminine side unless you are James.

Pat and James' interpretation seems like it could be spot on, especially as James dreamt of a maypole [page 133] which has a Ying Yang symbol on the top. Not that you can interpret dreams using New Age symbolism or anything like that…

EXCERPT FROM 40TH SESSION

JAMES, WHEN YOU CAME HERE NEARLY A YEAR AGO, OUR CONTRACT WAS TO EXPLORE STEALING.

I DON'T REALLY NEED TO COME HERE ANY MORE. I LIKE IT BUT I SHOULD BE AT WORK.

I HAVEN'T STOLEN OR FELT IN DANGER OF STEALING FOR A LONG TIME. I KNOW WHAT I MUST DO TO AVOID THE TRIGGERS NOW.

SO I'M WONDERING WHAT OUR CONTRACT IS NOW?

CONTRACT? I LIKE COMING TO SEE YOU AND HEARING WHAT YOU'VE GOT TO SAY. IT'S GOOD TO CHAT ABOUT MY WEEK AND THINGS...

A fantasy bond is a relationship tie that is based more on role playing and routine than on spontaneous interaction and genuine feelings.

For some, change is central to psychotherapy: changing engrained habits of thought and action and subsequently of feeling, as well as the transformative nature of the therapy relationship itself. Then there is the change of becoming a psychotherapy client followed by the change caused by ending the therapy relationship. Change can feel threatening and typically we can react with denial. How many times do we say, 'See you', when the likeliest outcome is, 'I'll never see you again'? Along with denial, regression is a common reaction to change. Regression is the abandonment of what has been most recently learned in favour of what was learned at an earlier stage of life. Here James is temporarily reverting to his old style of cocky-clever-school-boy with 'Isn't my money good enough for you?' For these and other reasons, a psychotherapy ending usually takes a few weeks to process.

Many therapists report on the phenomenon of having feelings about how useful or otherwise a client's significant others are to the client's personal growth. My feeling is that Pat approves of Juanita.

I'M HOPING YOU WON'T LOSE THE WORK WE'VE DONE TOGETHER. WORK THAT IS TOO PRECIOUS TO JEOPARDISE BY MY COMING TO YOUR WEDDING.

AND SEEING ME IN A DIFFERENT WAY MIGHT RISK IT TOO.

IF YOU RELAPSE OR WANT TO EXPLORE OTHER ISSUES, I EXPECT TO BE HERE FOR ABOUT 10 MORE YEARS.

YOU ARE NOT EVEN SAYING YOU'LL ALWAYS BE HERE.

THAT'S RIGHT.

I'D LIKE TO THINK I'LL ALWAYS SEE YOU AND YOU'LL ALWAYS BE HERE FOR ME.

DON'T YOU THINK THIS IS HARD FOR ME TOO JAMES? IT'S NOT JUST YOU WHO HAS FEELINGS ABOUT THIS ENDING.

THANKS FOR SAYING THAT.

It is hard for therapists to accept endings too, although they have more experience of them. Sometimes they can be tempted to enter into their clients' lives. It is usually a bad idea for all the reasons that are outlined by Pat. But if say, you wanted them to write an afterword for your graphic tale of psychotherapy, or something like that, they might consider it. It would just have to be considered very carefully.

Freud changed his mind about touch. In his early work, he used head and neck massage as he thought it aided age regression. However, gradually as he began to use free association and interpretation more, he became less keen on the use of touch in psychotherapy. He feared that using touch would gratify his patients' infantile needs and contaminate the transference. He also feared that touch might stimulate sexual feelings in both practitioner and patient. However, other practitioners, such as a contemporary of Freud's, Ferenczi, considered touch to be useful as a way of repairing early damage in patients. Freud and Ferenczi fell out about this and counsellors, psychotherapists and analysts have been falling out about it ever since.

An ending is an ending. An ending also heralds a new beginning.

AFTERWORD

A few weeks before being asked to write this afterword for *Couch Fiction*, I saw Ari Folman's notable anti-war film, *Waltz with Bashir*. At the showing, the director was asked why he had chosen animation as his medium for this documentary. He replied that it was the most fluid and effective way he could think of to show what was happening inside and outside people at the same time. He also pointed out that animation could reveal the gulf between what people showed on the surface and what they experienced inside. The words 'conscious' and 'unconscious' were not used, though the words 'surface' and 'depth' were. Folman praised the capacity of animation to leave a space for the audience to have their own emotional experience, without requiring that they identify with only one character or point of view. This capacity is in full evidence in Philippa Perry's unique and creative attempt to show, via the medium of the graphic novel, what happens in therapy. As a mature practitioner with a sceptical and enquiring mind, she clarifies for herself and for us too what the practice of therapy is really about.

Research has shown that success in therapy depends on the quality and strength of the relationship between the client and the therapist and an alliance that allows for both good and bad feeling. But which relationship are we talking about? This isn't a simple question. There is, of course, the conscious level relationship between the two people in the room. This is what enables the therapist to get trained and organise a safe space for the work. Here, we find the client's everyday capacity to choose to have therapy, get to their sessions, and pay for them.

In addition, each of them has a relation or connection to their own unconscious aspects. That's a further two important relationships to consider. The client's relationship to his unconscious is, basically, where the reasons for troubled behaviours, habits and feelings might be found. In the case of James, we see it in his early relationships with a withholding and self-centred mother and the emotional impact of this on him. On the other side, the therapist's relationship to her unconscious is where all those things that were supposed to have been addressed in her own personal training therapy might be found. Which means, of course, that there'll be a lot there that weren't addressed or found. Such things can easily sabotage subsequent work with her clients. For example, if Pat's background had made her unbearably envious of upper-middle-class life or the security of a profession like the law, her sensitivity to James's shame would be jeopardised. What if she too had not been taken seriously, in a full emotional sense, by her family? Might this not cloud her judgement with respect to James's problems? What if she too had a mother or a father who regarded her as a source of pride rather than as a person in her own right? We often find things in the therapist's inner world, present and past, that might slow up or sabotage the work. And, never to be forgotten, her unconscious is where the sources of empathy and compassion that are so important to the process are located as well. A therapist in part understands her client by understanding herself.

We are not yet done with the complex layers of the therapeutic relationship... There is going to be an unconscious relationship between therapist and client, going on in some isolation from the conscious working relationship. This is where clinical intuitions and useful fantasies about the work are to be found. Freud used the metaphor of a radio transmitter and radio receiver to explain how it is that things crop up in the mind of the therapist which may belong to the client (he was less interested in the vice versa but this has changed since then). The idea of unconscious to unconscious – what people now call 'right brain to right brain' – communication is central to most accounts of what makes therapy work. So, up to now, four relationships. Enough? No, because there are the relationships between the client's unconscious and the therapist's conscious mind, and between the therapist's unconscious and the client's conscious mind. Each partner is projecting a good deal of stuff into the other partner and this is neither good nor bad – it just is the case. This brings the number of relationships

within the therapy relationship to six and they can all happen at the same time. Readers may find it interesting to see how many of these relationships are shown to be active at any one time in this story.

That's just thinking about the story from a psychodynamic perspective. The tale is also open to being viewed through the lens of other perspectives – for example, humanism, existentialism and even behaviourism. Pat appears to integrate a number of theoretical approaches into her work. As we see on page 44, attachment theory is underpinning her questioning when she is asking James about his childhood. On page 73, she is showing an awareness of body-orientated therapy when she asks him to experiment with his breathing. Like a Gestaltist [page 88], we see her working with awareness in the here and now, and her 'process chart' and homework setting [page 89] appear to be borrowed from behavioural approaches. Underpinning it all, Pat usually has belief and confidence in what she is doing and, as Philippa Perry points out in her notes [page 89], it is possible that a placebo effect is there in the mix as well.

At this point, I need to say a few words about sex. There are many aspects to the sexual transference-countertransference in therapy. I have always said that if someone says that they fancy you, it is almost impossible not to be stirred, even in the tiniest sense, in response. This is quite normal. Even if the client is not the therapist's usual cup of tea, this reciprocal erotic response takes place and I wish it were more widely recognised. In James' and Pat's case, I think James' sexual fantasy is useful not only in terms of his ability to recover a kind of spontaneous masculinity that he had been conditioned to repress by his upbringing, but also because its symbolism speaks directly of his need to be recognised as having his own autonomous power and not be the plaything or puppet of a powerful mother. Yet what I have just written about the utility of James' sexual fantasy does not go deep enough. You see, like it or not, some kind of physical warmth between two people (call it sexual if you will) seems to be a necessity or precondition for the emotional growth and development of both of them. I guess the template is the parent-child relationship or other close relationship in the family. This is not incest (though tragically, the process I am describing does sometimes get abused). No, this is Eros in its widest sense – the Greek God inspiring a psychological principle of connectedness, relatedness, growth and transformation – life! Eros could be seen as a fertility god or a god of intercourse and conception, but he is also the flow of natural energy in connection. Nothing could be more innocent and more healing. So, when you watch what is happening between James and Pat, you will notice some mutual attraction, but also be aware of what Eros is adding to the mixture beyond its own fleshiness.

Despite all the research on therapeutic outcomes, there is no consensus about what the essential catalysts are for therapeutic change. Some people still feel it is the insight that accurate and well-timed interpretations bring. Others, that the new experience of therapy provides an environment for processes of growth and development, even on the level of the brain. Others feel that blocks to conscious and cognitive control have led to bad habits which can be displaced. But there is no agreement, though many believe that it is the therapist who heals and not the method. Jung's alchemists – whom he saw as the precursors of modern therapists – did their smelly, chemical, physical work in a laboratorium. But, just off this, there was also a little cell called an oratorium. Here, they prayed for and meditated upon a successful outcome. And, true to the orthodoxies of their day, written above the door to the little oratorium were the words 'Deo concedente' – God willing. Nowadays, therapists would be uncomfortable at leaving the outcome up to God! But the point I want to make is that there is an unknowable and mysterious factor to take into account beyond the control of the therapist, no matter how skilled he or she may be.

I hope the book is read outside and inside the therapy world. I know that it will spark off debates about therapy in our society which we need to have. I can imagine groups of therapy trainees and students pouring over these pages, measuring themselves against Pat and learning from her – not only from what she does well but also from her mistakes. I can also imagine clients and potential clients using the book as a much-needed point of entry. Philippa's account of therapy manages to be both hot and cold at the same time. She is well aware that therapy is not like a calibrated machine but is always a unique mix of two personalities. So, this is in no way a therapy manual – it is way too provocative for that.

ANDREW SAMUELS
Professor of Analytical Psychology,
University of Essex, UK

RECOMMENDED FURTHER READING

Evans, K. and Gilbert, M.C. *An Introduction to Integrative Psychotherapy*, Palgrave Macmillan, 2004
Provides overview of integrative psychotherapy with a relational perspective.

Gay, P. *The Freud Reader*, Vintage, 1995
An anthology of Sigmund Freud's key writings.

Hefferline, R.F, Goodman, P. and Perls, F, *Gestalt Therapy*, The Julian Press Inc, 1958
The all encompassing textbook of Gestalt theory, including coverage of the ways in which we interrupt our contact with the world and discussion of self actualisation and self awareness.

Holmes, J. *The Search for the Secure Base*, Bruner-Routledge, 2001
A good book about attachment theory which also has a useful section on endings in psychotherapy.

Hubble, M.A., Duncan, B.L, Miller, S.D., *The Heart and Soul of Change*, American Psychological Association, 1999
A useful overview of research into what works in therapy.

Khan, M. *Between Therapist and Client: The New Relationship*, Henry Holt and Company, 1991
An all-round good primer on the use of relationship in psychotherapy. Also discusses transference, intersubjectivity and self disclosure.

Mann, D. *Erotic Transference and Countertransference: Clinical Practice in Psychotherapy*, Routledge, 1999
All therapists, regardless of their looks, need to be prepared for erotic transference.

Mitchell, S.A. and Aron, L. *Relational Psychoanalysis, Volume 14*, The Analytic Press, 1999
Aron, L. and Harris, A. *Relational Psychoanalysis, Volume 15*, The Analytic Press, 2005
Collected academic papers on the relational process. Recommended for all practitioners of any type of talking therapy for bringing clarity and wisdom to a complicated process. Also recommended for interested parties of an academic bent.

Orbach, S. *The Impossibility of Sex: Stories of the Intimate Relationship Between Therapist and Patient*, Scribner, 2000
Fictional case studies from the therapist's point of view.

Yalom, I.D. *Love's Executioner*, Penguin, 1991
Case studies on the therapeutic relationship using existential theory. Easy and entertaining to read.

THANKS

Thank you to all my clients and supervisees, as well as to all the participants of all the training and continual professional development groups I have belonged to over the years, to my colleagues and candidates on the viva MA examination boards, and to participants of any workshop or course I have run.

A very big thank you to the following individuals who have inspired or mentored me, supported or put up with me and have sometimes done all of the above: Grayson Perry, Flo Perry, Charlotte Troy, Pat Morrisey, Catherine Gray, Dorothy Charles, Stella Tillyard, Andrew Samuels, Maria Gilbert, Diana Smukler, Jacob Covey, Susan Boynton, Lizzie Harcourt, Cathy Elliot, Lynn Keane, Helen Healy, Oliver Bennet, Yolanda Vazquez, Jonny Phillips, Kate Hardie and Jacky Klein.

I also owe a huge debt of gratitude to Junko Graat, who illustrated this comic, not only for her artistic work but for her belief, her love, her care, her loyalty and her reassuring presence.

—Philippa Perry

BIOGRAPHIES

PHILIPPA PERRY is a psychotherapist, psychotherapy supervisor and a fine art graduate. She is married to the artist, Grayson Perry, and they have a daughter, Flo.

JUNKO GRAAT trained and worked as a product designer in Japan before coming to England to study European horticulture. Junko now works as a gardener.

ANDREW SAMUELS practises as a Jungian analyst and is Professor of Analytical Psychology at Essex University, UK. He holds visiting chairs at New York, London and Roehampton universities. He also works internationally as a political and organisational consultant. He is the author of many books, including Politics on the Couch.